What Do You Call an Ant?

Mary Mueller
Illustrated by Sandra Reed

LET'S GO! PRESS

First edition, 2017

Library of Congress Catalog Card Number: 2017909182
ISBN 978-0-692-90545-6

10 9 8 7 6 5 4 3 2 1
Printed in The United States

To learn more about Mary Mueller and her books, please visit www.AuthorMaryMueller.com.

Illustrations by Sandra Reed
The illustrations in this book are watercolors.
To learn more about Sandra Reed and her illustrations, please visit www.InspiredCreationsArt.com.

Let's Go! Press
Dallas, Texas
www.LetsGoPress.com

To order more copies,
please visit:
www.whatdoyoucallanant.com

Dedicated to Family

What do you call an ant that is very smart?

What do you call a very tall ant?

Giant

Did you know?

Some ant species can be as big as an inch and a half
and some as small as one twentieth of an inch.

1/20"   1 1/2"

What do you call an ant that smells really good?

Fragrant

Did you know?

When an ant finds food, it will take some back to the nest and leave a scent along the trail, so others can find the food and help bring it back. Each ant colony has its own scent—that way any intruder is quickly smelled out.

What do you call a really limber ant?

Pliant

What do you call an ant that notices everything?

Observant

Did you know?

Ants have two eyes with each eye being made up of many lenses, which help them see movement very well. However, their vision is so poor that some insects have learned that if they stay perfectly still, the ants will never see them and pass right by rather than attack them.

What do you call an ant that leans when it stands?

Slant

Did you know?

Ants that live on trees can walk upside down on the underside of leaves. They have tiny, hooked claws at the ends of their feet that help them cling to rough surfaces.

What do you call an ant with a trunk?

Elephant

What do you call an ant that spends all her time in the garden?

Plant

Did you know?
Ants move A LOT of dirt. It is estimated that they move about fifty tons of dirt each year in one square mile.

What do you call an ant that comes from another country?

Immigrant

Did you know?

Red fire ants were accidentally brought to Alabama by cargo ships coming from South America in the 1930s. The ships needed something heavy to balance their loads, so soil was brought on board. Unbeknownst to the shippers, the ants got a free ride to the USA as they rode along in the soil. The aggressive ants quickly spread to nine states and gained a reputation for being a real pest because of their stinging bite and the damage they caused to both plant and animal life.

What do you call a really lively ant?

Exuberant

What do you call
a really colorful ant?

Vibrant

Did you know?

Like people, ants come in many different colors: black, brown, red, yellow, orange, or a combination of those colors. Some ants even have semi-transparent abdomens that take on the color of whatever it is they are eating.

What do you call a baby ant?

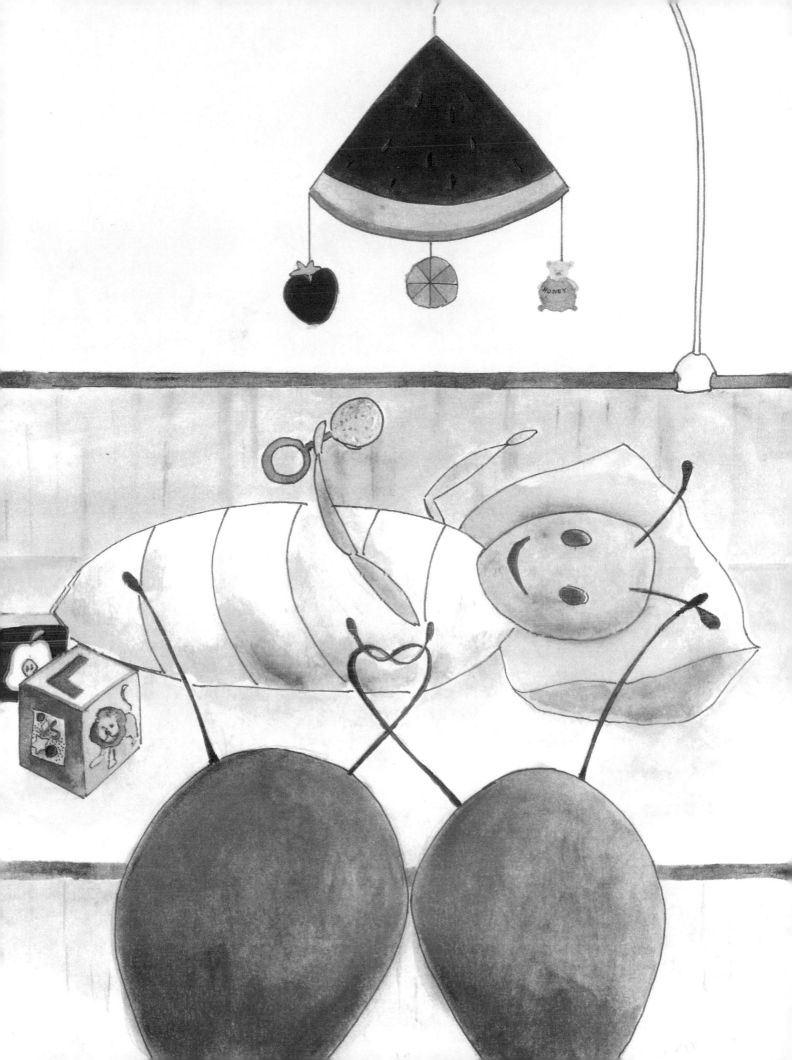

Infant

Did you know?

Ants lay eggs that hatch into larvae, which are soft and look a little bit like worms. The larvae are fed continually by adult ants and grow very fast to the pupa stage. The pupa will spin a cocoon around itself and stay in the cocoon until it is done changing. It comes out of the cocoon as an ant. Most ants only live forty-five to sixty days, but some ant species can live for several years.

What do you call a really happy ant?

Jubil**ant**

Did you know?

When carpenter ants find food, they not only leave a scented trail for other ants to find it, but they also do a "happy dance" when they return to the nest to let others know they should follow them back. The hungrier they are, the more excited they will dance!

What do you call a really brave ant?

Valiant

Did you know?

Some ant species have "soldier" ants. These ants protect their nest by blocking the entrance with their heads, which are shaped to match the opening. When a member of the nest returns, it touches the antennae of the guard ant to let it know it belongs to the colony. If it is an enemy, the guard ant does not move its head.

What do you call your favorite aunt?

Draw or paste a picture of your favorite aunt here.

TIA
Shanin

TIA
Cristen!!!

From...chloe